Sammy the Snail

Sammy the Snail

Copyright © 2022 by Faiza Pirmohamed

ISBN: 9788202491819 (Hardcover)

First Edition: 2022

TO WHICHEVER CHILD IS READING THIS,

I PRAY YOU ALWAYS BE

HAPPY,

HEALTHY AND

FREE FROM ANY HARM.

LOVE, MOM.

DON'T FORGET HOW SPECIAL YOU
TRULY ARE,

AND KNOW THAT YOU ARE LOVED
BY THOSE NEAR AND FAR.

A CHILD'S EMOTIONAL WELL-BEING IS AS
IMPORTANT AS THEIR PHYSICAL.

ONCE YOU REALISE HOW MUCH YOUR CREATOR LOVES YOU, THERE IS NOTHING THAT YOU WON'T BE ABLE TO GO THROUGH.

Sammy the Snail wandered excitedly around, trying not to disturb others from making a sound..

Today was yet again another sunny bright day, but Sammy still didn't want to play.

Instead, he kept on thinking about what he always thought of, and again he asked himself, "Where is my Creator? I look up and down, all around, but yet, my Lord still isn't found."

Activity 1

Look around you and write down 5 things made by your wonderful Creator!

Here is my list of 5 wonderful things my Creator made that I see around me!

1.

2.

3.

4.

5.

Sammy then decided that he had thought and searched alone for too long.

He needed some help from his nearest friends.

So, off he went, singing his favourite song.

Activity 2

List 5 things that make you feel good.

5 things that make me feel good:

1.

_____

2.

_____

3.

_____

4.

_____

5.

_____

On his way, he found Ruby the Rabbit.

"Ruby, Ruby," called out Sammy,
"Can you help me with a huge
favour? I need to know - where is my
Creator?"

Ruby thought and searched hard, but could not see, so she suggested that they go for a cup of tea.

While they were having their tea,
Ruby proposed that they imagine her
best place to be, which for her was by
the sea.

Activity 3

Think of your favourite place(s) to be! What do you see, hear and feel? List 5 things that you can reveal.

My favourite place(s) to be is:

· ·

I feel

· ·

· ·

· ·

· ·

I see

· ·

· ·

· ·

· ·

I hear

· ·

· ·

On their way, they found Mia the Monkey.

"Mia, Mia" they called, "Can you help us with a huge favour? We need to know – where is our Creator?"

Mia looked all around her and suddenly thought she had finally caught sight, but then changed her mind and decided they go for a quick bite.

While they were eating, Mia felt worried about not knowing the answer (but we all know that worrying never helps!). So, she recommended they all sit together and do what she normally did when she was feeling worried or stressed.

Mia suggested they breathe in and out with 10 slow breaths, using their chest. They could now clearly see, breathing in and out, helped them be in the present moment - which was the best place to be!

Activity 4

Take a deep breathe in: You will feel your chest go up. Hold it for about 5 seconds before exhaling. Try this as many times as you like. How does this make you feel?

Add a tick mark after each feeling you got after doing this activity!

Calm ☐

Relaxed ☐

Strong ☐

Happy ☐

Grateful ☐

Focused ☐

On their way they found Adam the Anteater.

"Adam, Adam" they called, "Can you help us with a huge favour? We need to know - where is our Creator?"

Adam had never thought of this before, but Erick the Elephant would know, that he was sure.

Activity 5

Think of the people that you know that you can trust and who would have the answers to your hardest questions. Know that you are truly loved and cherished by these people. Why are you thankful for them in your life? Can you think of 5 things that make you grateful for them?

Who am I grateful for in my life?

....

Why am I grateful for them?

1.

2.

3.

4.

5.

While they were on their way, they found Betty the Butterfly.

Betty said hi, and since they didn't notice her, she started feeling shy, "What happened to you?" They gasped... "You were a long, fuzzy caterpillar, and now you have changed. Was this a surprise, or was it pre-arranged?

Your bright, blue wings are ever so pretty. You are up so high - I bet you can see the entire city!"

Betty then spread her large, beautiful wings and said she wanted to explain some things:

"Life is full of surprises, but always comes with little gifts. I love to fly, but I also enjoyed the climb, that I won't deny. No matter how we are created, we are special indeed, and so we should always try to notice our God-given gifts to help us succeed. Come along now, we need to find Eric the Elephant, our next friend, there is always something new to learn and comprehend."

Activity 6

Life can always bring about an unknown surprise, but with that, a special gift can arise. Can you think of 5 traits you have that make you proud?

5 traits I am proud of in myself are:

Trait 1:

_____

Trait 2:

_____

Trait 3:

_____

Trait 4:

_____

Trait 5:

_____

They went to find Erick the Elephant
by the lake, and surely there he was,
drinking some water and tasting a
piece of cake.

"Erick, Erick" they called, "Can you
help us with a huge favour? We need
to know - where is our Creator?"

"Well then, my dear friends, have a seat, it could take a while before my speech ends."

They all sat around anxiously waiting for the elephant to speak and tried to stay quiet by not making a squeak.

"As I was saying..." said the Elephant, "Take a good look all around you, the proof is evident within us too.

All magnificence that you so clearly see, was neither made by you nor me. Our Creator made it all, as nothing for Him is too difficult or small.

Don't ever doubt or have fear,
because the Creator is always near.
Our Lord is everywhere we go, even if
you try to hide high or low.

God's beauty is scattered all around,
so that you can see the proof even
without hearing a sound.

From the tiny grass to the tall tree, it was all created by the Lord for you and me. We need to fill our hearts with kindness and love, and never forget that the Creator is always watching over us from above.

The road ahead may seem very long, but we can stay united and forever strong."

Sammy and his friends were delighted to hear. They knew that they were deeply loved and very special. No longer did they feel lost or have any fear.

Everywhere they looked, they could now see God's beauty and observe, which made them feel thankful and want to serve.

They had a purpose, so they started to become extra helpful and to everyone kind, and because of this they found something extraordinary, which was peace of mind.

Activity 7

Think of 5 things you can do today that will help someone and in turn make you feel fine and help you shine!

What are five things I can do to help someone today?

1. _____

2. _____

3. _____

4. _____

5. _____

Activity 8

Can you think of a time when you helped someone in need and how that made you feel? List 5 things about yourself that are special and great indeed!

Something I did to help someone in need:

. . . .

How that made me feel:

. . . .

Five things that are special and great about myself are:

1. _____

2. _____

3. _____

4. _____

5. _____

About the Author

Faiza was born in Birmingham, England. She came to Ontario, Canada, where she settled down after getting married. She sought to have a balanced life in terms of family and career and equally sought a career that could involve science as well as helping others.

This led her towards choosing pharmacy, which gave her an enhancing career while raising a young family. Faiza also had a deep passion and gravitated towards the Arts, as it gave her appreciation for an omnipotent Creator.

She enjoys reading, poetry and painting, as it is personally meditating and fulfilling. This led her onto a journey of writing stories and poems during her spare time; ultimately leading her to write this book.

She would like to thank her parents and husband for their unconditional love and support, and her three children, who taught her how to love unconditionally.